Pollution

Sally Morgan

Published in 2009 by Evans Brothers Ltd, 2A Portman Mansions,
Chiltern St, London WIU 6NR

Editor: Nicola Edwards
Designer: D.R. Ink
Photography: Ecoscene

British Library Cataloguing in Publication Data

Morgan, Sally
Pollution. - (Helping our planet)
1. Pollution - Juvenile literature 2. Pollution prevention -
Juvenile literature
I. Title
363.7'3

ISBN: 9780237536510

Printed in Dubai

Picture Credits:
Title Judyth Platt; Contents Angela Hampton; P6 Vicki Coombs; P7 Dave Ellison; P8 Judyth Platt; P9 Alan Towse; P10 Erik Schaffer; P11 Pat Groves; P12 Jon Bower; P13 Chinch Gryniewicz; P14 Wayne Lawler; P15 Graham Neden; P16 Erik Schaffer; P17 Roy Langstaff; P18 Steve Kazlowski; P19 Andrew Brown; P20 Kieran Murray; P21 Visual and Written; P22 Wayne Lawler; P23 Edward Bent; P24 David Wootton; P25 Peter Landon; P26 Angela Hampton; P27 John Famer; P29 Graham Neden

Printed on chlorine free paper from sustainably managed sources.

Contents

Harming the planet 6
Dirty air 8
Cars everywhere 10
Cleaning the air 12
Ozone 14
Polluted water 16
Cleaning up the rivers 18
Oil spills 20
Digging and dumping 22
Farming and pollution 24
Cleaning up the planet 26
Glossary 28
Index 30

Harming the planet

We all need clean air to breathe, clean water to drink and a safe place to live. If the air, water and land around us are polluted, this can harm our health and the health of other animals and plants.

Oil spills can harm sea birds such as this guillemot.

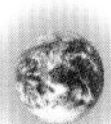

People pollute the environment every day. We can see some pollution, such as rubbish floating on water, and smoke coming out of a chimney. Some pollution is invisible. For example, some factories send harmful gases into the air.

Find out more

Think about the area where you live. What activities might pollute your local environment? Think about rubbish, smoke and transport. To find out more about pollution visit http://tiki.oneworld.net/pollution/pollution4.html.

▼ Power stations and factories sometimes cause pollution that we can see.

Dirty air

People pollute the air in many ways. When we burn fuels, such as coal and oil, they release gases. The gases include carbon dioxide and sulphur dioxide. Sulphur dioxide mixes with water in the atmosphere to make acid rain.

Acid rain has damaged this tree.

What can be done?

Today many countries have laws that prevent factories and people from producing these harmful gases. For example, in some cities people are not allowed to light a coal fire or have a bonfire.

When acid rain falls on trees and other plants it damages their leaves. It may even kill them. Acid rain damages stone buildings too, wearing away the stone.

When trees are damaged by acid rain they lose their leaves. Then there is less food for animals such as this koala.

Cars everywhere

Many of us use cars to take us to school or work, to the shops or on holiday. Cars, buses and lorries pollute the air with waste gases and soot. These exhaust fumes spoil the air, and they can make breathing difficult.

Cars damage the environment in other ways too.

A thick layer of smog hangs over Malaga in southern Spain. Smog is a mix of fog and the pollution from cars.

We breathe in the soot and gases from car exhausts.

More cars mean more roads. When we build new roads we use up more countryside. Then the places where plants and animals live may be damaged or destroyed.

You choose

Make a diary of all your journeys for a week. How many bus or car journeys did you make? How many times did you walk or cycle? How do you like to travel best when you can choose?

Cleaning the air

There are many ways to make the air around us cleaner. Factories pollute the air but we can make laws to stop the pollution. For example, power stations can be forced to use air filters inside chimneys to remove sulphur dioxide before it reaches the air.

What can be done?

Smoking cigarettes pollutes the air and harms our health. Many countries now ban people from smoking in public places.

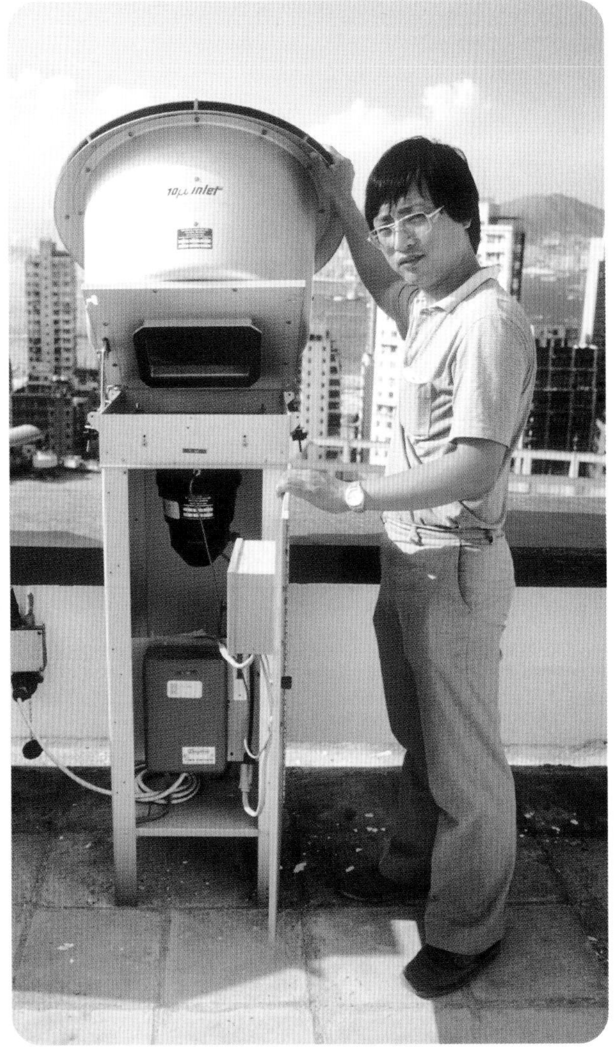

This man is checking levels of air pollution in Hong Kong. The machine sucks in air and shows how clean or dirty it is.

We can make cars cleaner too. People can remove harmful gases in the exhaust by fitting a device called a catalytic converter. New designs of cars are much cleaner than old ones. For example, new electric cars have a motor instead of an engine. This makes them quieter and cleaner.

This electric car is being charged using electricity from solar panels.

Ozone

High in the atmosphere that surrounds our planet is a layer of gas called the ozone layer. The ozone layer stops harmful ultraviolet (UV) rays in sunlight from reaching the ground. Ultraviolet light can harm people's eyes and cause skin cancers. It also harms wildlife.

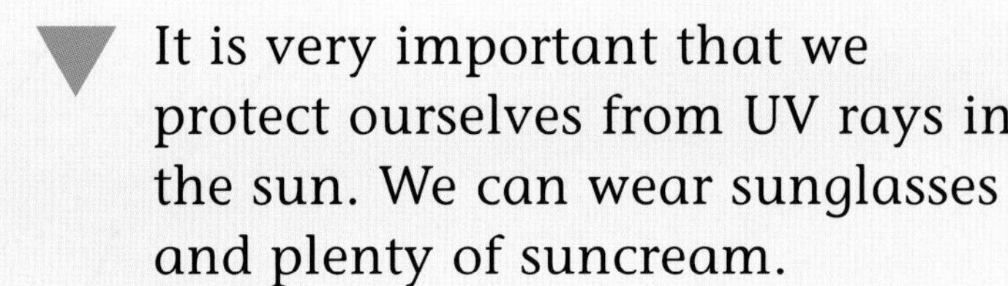

It is very important that we protect ourselves from UV rays in the sun. We can wear sunglasses and plenty of suncream.

Scientists measure the amount of ozone in the atmosphere above Antarctica.

People are damaging the ozone layer with chemicals. They use these chemicals in spray cans and fridges. The chemicals are now banned, but they are still in the atmosphere. This means the ozone layer is still being damaged.

Find out more

Each year a 'hole' forms in the ozone layer above Antarctica, which lets UV light through. Find out more about the ozone hole and the work of the scientists in the Antarctic at http://www.antarctica.ac.uk/.

Polluted water

People have dumped their waste into rivers and oceans for hundreds of years. This waste includes sewage, rubbish, and factory waste.

Waste water from a factory in Spain is being pumped into the Mediterranean Sea.

You choose

You can choose to avoid polluted beaches when you're on holiday. How do you know if the water at the beach is clean enough to swim in? Around the world many beaches fly a Blue Flag. This shows people that the water in the sea is clean.

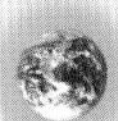

The waste harms the animals that live in the water because they need clean water to survive. Animals may eat the rubbish by mistake or they may become trapped in it.

Sewage from toilets is harmful too because it contains bacteria that can cause disease.

This diver has been removing litter from the sea. She found plastic bags, aluminium drink cans and other pieces of rubbish.

Cleaning up the rivers

Many rivers are becoming cleaner. Some countries have strict laws about the type of waste that people can empty into rivers and oceans. The waste has to be cleaned first so that it is safe to enter the water.

Salmon like clean water and are the first fish to disappear when the water is polluted. Now they are returning to some rivers.

What can be done?

We can use plants called reeds to treat sewage. People pump sewage into shallow reed beds. The water flows around the reeds and comes out clean.

In some places, people clean dirty water and sewage in treatment plants. The polluted water is pumped into huge tanks where the solids sink to the bottom and are removed. Then people clean the remaining water before releasing it into local rivers.

Oil spills

Every day tankers carry oil around the world. Each tanker holds thousands of litres of oil. When an accident happens oil spills into the water. Nearby beaches are covered in thick black oil. Animals such as birds and seals may be covered in oil too (look back at the picture on page 6).

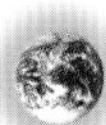

What can be done?

New laws say that people who build tankers now have to make them with two hulls, one inside the other. This means that there is less chance of oil leaking after an accident.

We can clean oil from beaches with jets of water and detergent, but it is a messy job. We can save the lives of oiled animals, too. People help to clean the birds and look after them until they are well enough to be released back into the wild.

Find out more

There is more information about how we can help injured and oiled animals on this website: http://www.ibrrc.org.

Digging and dumping

Most of the Earth's resources, such as coal, oil, iron and copper, are in the ground. People cause pollution when they dig up these resources.

This stream in Australia has been polluted by water from an old mine.

We can plant trees on land that has been polluted by mining.

People dig huge quarries to remove rocks such as limestone and granite. They dig long tunnels underground to remove coal and dump the waste rock nearby.

What can be done?

We can clean up old quarries and mines and replant the land with trees and other plants. Soon wildlife moves back.

 Farming and pollution

Crops need lots of nutrients to grow well, so farmers add fertilisers to the soil. Farmers spray plants with liquids that kill pests and weeds. All these substances can harm the environment.

This machine is spraying a crop with a mixture of liquid chemicals. The liquid will kill any bugs that might want to eat the plants.

Farmers can grow vegetables without using any harmful substances.

Organic farmers do not use pest and weed killers. They use natural methods to control pests and diseases.

You choose

Organic farming is better for the environment but the harvests are smaller. If every farmer farmed organically there would not be enough food for everyone. What is more important, the environment or food for people?

Cleaning up the planet

There are many ways we can help to clean up our environment. If we reduce the amount of electricity we use, we will burn less coal, gas and oil in power stations. Remember to turn off lights, computers and televisions when they are not in use, to turn down the heating, and use low energy equipment.

Turning down the heating by just one degree can help us to save energy at home and at school.

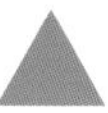

These children in India are walking to school. It is much better for the environment to walk to school rather than to go by car.

If we make fewer car journeys, there will be fewer cars on the road and less fuel will be burnt. Rather than go by car, see if you can walk, or cycle instead. This will help to reduce pollution - and it's better for your health too! Find out if your school has a 'walk to school' scheme.

What can be done?

Many groups run clean-up days to clear rubbish from beaches and river banks. See if you can help on one of these days.

Glossary

acid rain rain that is more acid than normal because of pollution, especially sulphur dioxide

atmosphere the layer of gases that surrounds the Earth

bacteria tiny organisms. Some bacteria cause disease

carbon dioxide a colourless and tasteless gas in the air. We breathe out carbon dioxide

catalytic converter a device fitted to the exhaust of a car to remove harmful gases

chemicals substances produced by a reaction or process

exhaust hot gases that leave the engine of a vehicle

fertiliser a substance rich in nutrients that is added to soil to help crops to grow

guillemot a sea bird with black and white feathers

hull the outer shell of a boat

hydrogen a type of gas that we can use as a fuel

motor a machine that can move something, for example an electric car has a motor that spins the wheels and moves the car

 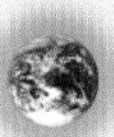

nutrients substances that help plants to grow well

organic crops that people grow without the use of chemicals

ozone layer a layer about 15 to 40 kilometres high in the atmosphere that is rich in ozone

pollution damage to the environment caused by substances that make the air, water or land dirty

sewage waste from toilets

smog a hazy layer that forms in the air above a city which is made up of smoke, fog and gases from vehicles and factories

solar panels panels that collect energy from the Sun and turn it into energy we can use

sulphur dioxide a gas that causes acid rain

treatment plant a place where dirty water goes through a process that makes it clean

ultraviolet invisible rays from the sun that can damage our eyes and skin

Index

Numbers in **bold** refer to pictures.

acid rain 8, **8**, 9, **9**
air 6, 7, 8, 12
animals 6, **6**, **9**, 17, **18**, 20, 21
atmosphere 8, 14, 15

bacteria 17
beaches 16, **16**, 20, **20**, 21, **21**, 27

carbon dioxide 8
cars 10, **10**, 11, **11**, 13, **13**, 27
catalytic converter 13
chemicals 15, 24, **24**
coal 8, 22, 23, 26

environment 7, 11, 24, 25, 26, 27

factories 7, 8, 12
farming 24, **24**, 25, **25**
fuels 8, 27

gases 7, 8, 10, 13, 14

health 6

land 6
laws 8, 12, 18, 21

oil 8, 20, **20**, 21, **21**, 22, 26
ozone layer 14, 15

plants 6, 9, **9**, 19, **19**, 23, **23**, 24, **24**, **25**
pollution 6, 7, **7**, 8, 10, **10**, **11**, 12, **12**, 13, 16, **16**, 18, **20**, **21**, 22, **22**, 23
power stations **7**, **8**, 12, 26

quarries 23

rubbish 16, 17

saving energy 26, **26**, 27
scientists 15, **15**
sewage 16, 17, 19
smog 10, **10**
smoking 12
solar panels 13, **13**
sulphur dioxide 8, 12

treatment plants 19

UV rays 14, **14**, 15

water 6, 7, 16, **16**, 17, **17**, 18, **18**, 19, **19**, 20, **20**, 21, **22**